To have and to hold

Roger Royle

Contents

Ellingham Church, Norfolk.

Anniversary celebrations

It doesn't matter whether you are celebrating your first wedding anniversary or your seventy-first, it is still very much a cause for celebration. You can look back to the day when you first met; the day when you decided to get married; the day you got married. You can get out the photographs, the tape recording, even the video and recall the many happy minutes of each hour of your wedding day.

Doubtless there'll be laughter as you remember what you looked like. There may even be hysterics when you remember what your favourite aunt looked like. There may well be a few tears as you see people who were so much a part of that day and so much a part of your life who are no longer with you. There could even be a few regrets as you think of people that you left out and later wished had been there. Or regrets when you recall situations that occurred, even words that were said which nearly upset what was otherwise a wonderful day.

But at anniversary time your thoughts are of happiness and thanksgiving. The partner whom you chose and who chose you is still with you. You have both been faithful to those vows, the most important vows that you have ever taken: your wedding vows. Anniversary time can also be a wonderful opportunity for taking another look at those vows. And wherever you were married, in church or Registrar's office, the vows would have been basically the same. So let's take a look.

A mystical union

Although you may have been as cool as a cucumber on your wedding day, when you reached the actual place for the marriage ceremony your heart doubtless started to flutter. All the things that you had been told about the occasion went from your head and all you wanted to do was get into that building and get on with it.

It is now, as you look back, that you can appreciate the total meaning of the marvellous occasion in which you were a principal player. You can realise that the contract you made with the person you love is not just a legal bond written down on a piece of paper and signed by both of you and a couple of witnesses. It is also a mystical union which reflects the union that is between Christ and his Church. The Church is seen as the Body of Christ here on earth. It is a relationship which is deeply spiritual. It is a union which, in its relationship with God, transcends human understanding. And the bond that you have with your partner is part of that mystical union.

It does us no harm whatsoever to realise that at times we can't understand everything. We need to accept that there are special relationships that can't be explained, analysed or dissected. The bond of love that keeps the two of you together can't be put under a microscope: it is of course very real but it is also mystical. And that mystical union is the same as the union that Christ has for his Church. It's quite awe-inspiring.

God, the best maker of all marriages,
Combine your hearts in one.
Shakespeare

The Abbey Church Yard, Bath.

Commended in holy writ

It is always good to know, when you are embarking on something new, that someone has been there before you: it gives you that extra sense of security. The marriage service reminds us of a wedding that took place in Cana of Galilee.

The occasion was not without problems for during the reception they ran short of drink. But the hosts were very fortunate because amongst the guests was Jesus. Hearing of their problem, he ordered six stone jars to be filled with water. Having filled them the servants were then told to draw some of the water out and to take it to the steward of the feast. When the steward drank it he was amazed and even asked the bridegroom where the wine had come from; he also commented that most people, when they are serving wine, begin with the good stuff and gradually let the standard deteriorate! But not this time: the good wine had been kept to the last. This was in fact the first recorded miracle that Jesus did.

It is a miracle that should repeat itself within every marriage since each one begins as water: it is ordinary, it is useful. But in time the water of the early days is turned into wine, and vintage wine at that. There may well be times when it changes back to water, but as long as there is that miracle ingredient of love within the marriage it will turn back again into wine.

Unadvisedly, lightly or wantonly

Doubtless many times you were told that you had to go into marriage with both eyes wide open. At a time like that it's no good closing your eyes or even putting on rose-tinted spectacles. What you need to do is to be able to see as clearly as you possibly can and as much as you possibly can. And this is why you were told not to undertake marriage unadvisedly, lightly or wantonly.

A person is very arrogant indeed if they never seek advice. And the more important the decision the greater the need for sound advice. So you need to choose your adviser carefully. There is no point in the blind leading the blind. Good advice is invaluable and a good adviser remains a firm friend for life. This is as it should be, because so often we want and need to use advisers time and time again.

The warning not to undertake marriage lightly or wantonly is a warning that should stay with you throughout your married life. There is always the lighter side to marriage as there is a lighter side to life, but as an institution there could be nothing more serious than marriage. It is, after all, a very great commitment. Nor can marriage really be seen as a wanton act. The word 'wanton' brings with it many different meanings including undisciplined, ungoverned and rebellious. And none of these describe a sound, secure, loving relationship like marriage.

Soberly and in the fear of God

When you were dressed up in your expensive clothes and a small fortune had been paid out on cars, flowers, photographers and food, the last thing that you wanted to be reminded was that the ceremony you were about to take part in was to be undertaken soberly and in the fear of God. Obviously, 'soberly' was not just referring to an excess of alcohol, but it is a useful reminder that many a celebration has been brought to a tearful end by people who have not been able to drink wisely. Sadly, many a marriage has floundered for that very same reason. Drinking excessive alcohol may only be the outward sign of what is an inner turmoil, but it has the power to destroy.

To describe someone as a sober person doesn't necessarily mean that they're teetotal; it's just another way of describing their wisdom. Nor does it mean that they're dull or boring. The sober person also realises that living in the fear of God is not a threat, it is a privilege. Fear – when it refers to God – is the sign of respect, of wonder, of humility. It is the sign which shows that you are fully aware that there is a power greater than you on whom you are dependent, and to whom you are responsible. But there is a great difference between this power and earthly powers because the force behind this power is the force of love. And so living in the fear of God is also living in the love of God, and it is that love which you try to reflect in your marriage.

An honourable estate

Marriage is often described in many different ways, some of which are none too flattering. But the description of it as 'an honourable estate' is one which has great dignity. No relationship can survive without dignity, and certainly marriage is no exception. A lot of the time it may seem as though there is very little dignity in marriage as you make sure that you have a roof over your heads, clothes for your bodies and food for your stomachs. When you, your partner, your children and the house look a mess it is quite difficult to remember that marriage is an honourable estate. But it is.

Within the solemnity of the marriage ceremony there is the dignity which is an integral part of your marriage. But so is there dignity within the humour and happiness of the occasion. An honourable estate is not always a solemn one: it is solemn when it needs to be solemn; it is bubbling when it needs to bubble. But it always gets its timing right. A relationship soon loses dignity if it isn't sensitive to the mood of each occasion and of each other.

Honour, respect and dignity go hand in hand and they make a wonderful trio. Sadly they are not free gifts as they so often have to be worked very hard for. But once they are there within a marriage they provide foundations on which is built an honourable estate.

> *Marriage the happiest bond of love might be,*
> *If hands were only joined when hearts agree.*
>
> Lansdowne

Silent Valley, Co. Down.

The Valley of Rock, Lynton, Devon.

Instituted of God Himself

When things are not going too well within the family, money is short, the children are quarrelling, and the roof is leaking, you must wonder who thought up this whole idea of marriage in the first place. The answer is God.

The bond that God created between Adam and Eve was a very close one indeed. As the story goes in Genesis, after God had created all the animal kingdom along with the birds of the air and the fishes of the sea, He felt that Man needed a companion. And so God caused the man to go into a deep sleep and while he was asleep God took a rib from the man and out of it created woman. The pattern of marriage was then created according to Genesis by the man leaving his father and mother and cleaving to his wife so that they become one flesh.

The creation story in Genesis is seen by different people in different ways, but however it is interpreted it shows the need that man has for woman and the need woman has for man. It also shows how precious that relationship is in the eyes of God, and that it is so precious that it even takes precedence over the relationship that a parent has for their child. Your marriage will always have something very unique about it, because you are both unique individuals. But you will also have the joy of knowing that marriage itself is not unique as it is part of God's eternal plan for creation.

Any impediment?

There is always that intake of breath and a slight loss of colour in the cheeks by both bride and groom when they hear the congregation asked on their wedding day if they know or any just cause or impediment why this couple should not be married. I expect you remember it well: it is always the moment when somebody in their wisdom decides to cough and the couple think the end of the world is only minutes away. The only impediments that can be legally claimed are that one – or both – of the couple is already married or they are too closely related. After all, a man may not marry his grandmother and a grandfather can't marry his granddaughter. But this doesn't stop there being other impediments. Hopefully by the time you reached the altar they were well and truly ironed out, but sometimes they have a nasty habit of lingering and anniversary time can be a very good opportunity to sort them out.

Impediments come in all sizes. There are the silly little irritating habits like leaving the cap off the toothpaste or never wiping the bath. There are the slightly more serious ones such as forgetting to say when you will be late home or making arrangements without consulting one another. And there are the very serious impediments like lack of trust and dishonesty. These are impediments which must be removed, and the sooner, the better.

St John's College, Cambridge.

To have and to hold

Doubtless if you had hymns at your wedding you chose them with great care. They were most probably ones that meant a lot to you or you had heard them at another wedding and liked them a lot. Sometimes the hymns are passed down from generation to generation; what mother had, daughter wants. The tunes chosen to dance to at the reception or party in the evening are normally the ones that the DJ is able to supply. But wise DJs make sure that they are able to supply music suitable for all tastes and all ages. One of the most suitable songs is of course 'All of me why not take all of me'. How well those words reflect the promise 'To have and to hold'.

To have and to hold implies two things: possession and protection. Protection is marvellous and within a true marriage great trouble is taken by the partners to protect one another from things that may hurt them. And this protection is of course extended when children arrive on the scene. Children, after all, have a right to protection. Possession is also wonderful, for with possession comes enjoyment. There is the thought that you have something worth having and that you intend to hold on to it for as long as you can. It is a possession whose actual worth can never really be measured because to you it means more than anything, and to hold that possession gives you the duty to protect and the privilege to be protected.

To comfort

Over the years some words have a nasty habit of changing their meaning. 'Comfort' is certainly one of them. Now 'comfort' tends to mean a warm fire, a pair of slippers, a good book and a general feeling that all is well with the world. But this is not what comfort originally meant. When a warrior wanted to encourage his soldiers to fight hard in battle it was often said that he 'comforted' his soldiers. This he might well have done by prodding his soldiers with swords and spears. Very few of us would find that comforting. The Holy Spirit is also often referred to as 'The Comforter' and yet the Holy Spirit is more likely to challenge you than to provide you with a pair of slippers.

The word 'comfort' originally meant 'keeping someone up to the mark' so no wonder it is a word associated with marriage. Keeping one another up to the mark should always be part of a happy marriage. It is no good taking care over everything before you get married, sustaining those standards for a few years after and then forgetting all about them. If anything, as a marriage develops so the standards should get higher. Standards don't just apply to outward appearances or materialistic possessions. They refer to the quality of life, the quality of care that each partner shows to the other. When these standards are high then life is very comfortable.

Upper Slaughter, Gloucestershire.

To keep

Every so often most families will have a good turn-out: papers and magazines that are no longer relevant are thrown out or, better still, sent to be recycled; toys that are no longer played with are hopefully found new homes; clothes that no longer fit or are thought to be unfashionable are sent to the charity shop to do some more good before they finally become threadbare. But whenever this clearing-out takes place some things are always kept and treasured. The pressure to throw things away has become very great. We live in a disposable society where cups, plates, knives and nappies are geared for what is assumed to be easier living. You don't wash and re-use: you throw away. This may of course be very convenient for things but it can never work with people – and it should never work with marriage.

The promise that is made 'to keep' is as binding as any of the other promises. It is a promise which should of course come naturally. When you have decided that there is one person to whom you wish to commit your life then the natural reaction is to want to keep that person for as long as you possibly can. They must be the one treasure which will not need to be recycled, will never go out of fashion nor need to be changed for a later model. Keeping someone also means caring for them. There is no point putting them 'in the attic' to be looked at occasionally. No, this person is kept so that they are a part of your whole life.

Never marry but for love, but see that thou lovest what is lovely.

William Penn

From this day forward

The start of something new is always exciting even if at times a little nerve-racking. There is the thrill of looking forward – but there is also the fear of the future. You never know what lies ahead and so naturally you are apprehensive, but if you never venture forward your life will become dull and close in upon itself.

With the words 'From this day forward' in the marriage ceremony you embarked on a great new venture, the greatest that you will ever undertake. But you embarked with determination. As you start something new you put the past behind you and you look to the future. You don't forget the past, because within it there were most probably many things from which you can learn, but you look to the future. It is impossible to see what lies ahead if you are constantly looking over your shoulder at the things you have passed; by looking back you just see things you have seen already and you are in great danger of not being prepared for the excitement that lies ahead.

It's a bit like runners at the start of a race. They may be crouched down ready to start, but the moment the gun is fired they are off with their eyes firmly fixed on what lies ahead. There is of course the occasional glance back, just to see how they how they are doing, but it is only occasional because the firm intention is to move forward. 'From this day forward' has the same feel about it: obviously there is no rush but this is the start of a journey into the future.

Tarbert, Harris, Highlands.

For better

When discussing anybody or anything it's always best to start with what is good about the person or the situation. After all, it was the good things about your partner that attracted you to them in the first place.

Both partners in a marriage should always focus on the good in each other and emphasise the positive. But at anniversary time there ought to be a special concentration on what is good as you prepare for another year together. The goodness in each one of you will always need encouraging, but this is well worth doing because it was that goodness that brought you together and made you decide that you wanted to be together for the rest of your lives. The thoughtfulness, the understanding, the care, the humour, the devotion and the integrity which you see in each other are all part of that goodness of character, which must never be taken for granted.

It is also excellent to remember the good times that you have had together: parties you have given, films you've seen, holidays you've spent, things you have bought – they are all part of the good times. And if there have been good times in the past there is no reason why there shouldn't be good times in the future. The routine obviously has to be kept going and often much of that routine will be enjoyable, but the good times – that extra sparkle – will always be the highlights which stand out in any relationship.

A good marriage is that in which each
appoints the other guardian of his solitude.
Rainer Maria Rilke

For worse

The wedding vows are totally realistic. Nobody can hope to stay on a high for twenty-four hours a day, seven days a week, fifty-two weeks a year: there are bound to be the down times. And this is why you need reminding constantly that you took your partner not just for better but also for worse.

Within each one of us there are characteristics which are not pleasant, which reflect the bad side of us. And sadly the day we get married these characteristics don't miraculously disappear. Jealousy, suspicion, possessiveness, deception are all deep-rooted feelings which must be faced. On your own they can often remain problems which may have tragic consequences but, faced together, you can cope. It will not be easy, and there is always the possibility that you will not be successful, but you have the duty to try.

It is also important to remember that, for every fault you are able to find in your partner, there is a strong possibility that one is lurking in you. Within any relationship there can be faults on both sides and just as it is important that you help your partner get over their weaknesses so it is vital that you take the trouble to ask for help yourself. It is no good either of you pretending that there is nothing wrong at all, or that in time it will go away. Because it won't. The only way of coping with what is worse in each one of us is to own up to it and to face up to it. From that start something better can be built.

For richer

Possibly the days when a prospective husband was asked 'What are your prospects?' have gone but many couples still try to make sure they have something in the bank before starting their married life. How long that money will remain untouched is another matter. With mortgages and children to support, the scales of the bank balance tend to be weighted in the downward direction. But the cash flow situation always needs careful attention.

Material wealth can of course be of great benefit to a marriage. It means that a house can be bought and furnished without too much stress. It means that holiday brochures can be explored with a view to booking something rather exciting. It means that children can be kept up-to-date with the latest in educational technology. It means that at the end of the month there is still something to draw on. If you share these benefits, rejoice and be thankful, but also remember that riches shared are often riches doubled. When riches increase you should not necessarily set your heart upon them, for you may be able to help relieve the poverty of others, and that too should bring you great happiness.

Riches should not always be measured in pounds and pence, or in possessions. Many people have a spiritual richness which is of far greater value than any material wealth. It is the richness of loving and knowing that you are loved. That is wealth indeed.

For poorer

There is a strong possibility that at one time or another in your married life you have experienced some sort of poverty. Just as riches are relative so is poverty: what is to one person a meagre crust, to another is a banquet. But coping with material poverty is not easy. So many of us come to put our trust in possessions. We even at times think that we are judged by our possessions and the material style in which we live, so that when cut-backs occur not only do we feel that it affects us, we also feel it affects the way others think of us.

But spiritual and emotional poverty are much more damaging. When the richness of your love begins to fade, the wealth of your care is reduced, then your marriage is put under pressures which must be faced and hopefully coped with. This may of course mean outside help is needed as we are not always able to understand why what was so rich emotionally has become so poor. And failure to get that help can mean that what was relatively poor becomes abject poverty. From poverty, however, can come strength, a new force that binds you together when, with determination, you set about facing the future. Poverty can make you fall back on your resources, which, although they may seem little at the time, can become the strength from which a new, richer life springs. When poverty is turned into riches, the riches are very great indeed.

The spirit of poverty is to live in the gladness of today.

Rule of Taizé

Portloe, Cornwall.

River Teign, Devon.

In sickness

On your wedding day you were doubtless as fit as a fiddle. There may have been the odd headache, there may well have been the slight uneasiness in the stomach, but apart from that you were fit and well. And for most of the early and middle years of your life this feeling of healthy well-being probably continued. But as old age approaches and you are not quite as young as you used to be, what was an odd twinge can become a debilitating pain. It isn't just the elderly who experience this. Disease does not respect either people or age, and illnesses like M.S., M.E., Motor Neurone disease, cancer or Parkinson's disease can make what was a very healthy life into one which is physically very limited.

For some people illness is very frightening. When they are ill themselves they feel lost and bewildered. When they see it in others they want to walk away from it as fast as they can. But this is exactly the time when help is needed more than ever. To be with someone who is seriously ill is very exhausting and extremely limiting: they make demands upon you, often unwillingly; they feel guilty because the last thing they ever wanted to be to you was a burden. But it is at a time like that when you are called to show the depth of your love.

The marriage vows are very real: they acknowledge the downs as well as the ups. But by showing your supportive, accepting love to your partner when things are down you have set about turning it into an up. Sickness, like poverty, can lead to greater strength.

In health

With the increasing number of health clubs, health checks, well-woman and well-baby clinics, it seems that health is high on the agenda in most people's minds. Flick through any magazine and you will generally find ways of keeping yourself in better trim. In fact, if you are not careful, health can become a god in its own right.

But it is important to remember that the body we have been given needs looking after. There are times when we stupidly think we are immortal: we push our bodies too hard and then we wonder why they rebel; we don't feed them with the right food: instead of a proper, balanced diet we grab what we can when we can; we drink and smoke with little regard for what it is doing to us in the long run; we sometimes take tablets which may remove discomfort in the short term but could possibly have adverse long term effects. We must remember that the body, like any machine, needs proper care and regular servicing.

If it's important that we look after the body it's also vital that we keep the mind and soul in proper working order. Minds and souls need feeding. The mind needs to be stimulated, to be taken down new avenues and to be made to be creative. The soul should also be stretched. The prayers that were part of our childhood will not do when in every other way we wish to be regarded as mature adults. When fed with music, with words, with silence and with wonder, the soul becomes the driving force in our lives, so it's vital it remains fit and well.

Cromford, Derbyshire.

Sennen, Cornwall.

To love

Love is seen as the foundation of every marriage – and so it should be. Without it a marriage stands little chance of surviving. But what is love?

There is no better definition of love than the one given by St. Paul in his first letter to the people of Corinth. At many a marriage service it is added as an extra lesson but because the words are so familiar their true value is often not appreciated. St. Paul points out that, in harsh reality, although you may have tremendous knowledge, great faith, immense charity and even the strength to move mountains, it means absolutely nothing if you have no love. It's quite a sobering thought that, unless love underpins our actions, even our faith isn't worth that much. St. Paul also makes it clear that love can cope with anything because it is never jealous, arrogant, boastful or rude. It does not always want its own way, nor is it irritable or resentful. And he goes on to point out that love bears all things, believes all things, hopes all things and endures all things. Love is able to do this because it is patient and kind. And it never ends.

What is also so important about true love is that it grows: it doesn't stay still. It always wants to reach out in new ways to show that it is such an important part of our lives. It is all these different ingredients that make love so special.

To cherish

Just as the word 'comfort' has changed its meaning over the years, so the word 'cherish' is one that is rarely heard these days. But it is a beautiful word, with a lovely sound to it. It means of course, as regards an idea, 'to harbour fondly' or, as regards a person, 'to hold dear or to care for tenderly'. Cherish is that soft, supportive word that encourages you to realise how precious a person is to you. It is the word that shows you really value them.

When they are valued for who they are rather than what they can do, people flourish. Being valued is the life blood that makes them grow. Obviously it is very important to be appreciated at the very outset of life because this is when patterns of life are set, but being valued must also be seen as a continuing process. The elderly person feels that they are of little value because they can no longer do the things they used to do, but here they are mistaken because it is who they are that is important, and it is who they are that is of value.

It's as important for the husband to cherish as the wife – even though it may be thought of as a rather feminine word. Tenderness needs to be practised by both men and women for it is a gift which can only come from strength. And those who think that, because the word 'cherish' is not used so frequently these days, it is of little value have made a very big mistake.

There is a time when a man distinguishes
the idea of felicity from the idea of wealth;
it is the beginning of wisdom.

R.W. Emerson

Norwich Cathedral as seen from Mousehold Heath.

To obey

You can always guarantee that at one point during the marriage service the congregation will become very attentive indeed. It is during the bride's vows, and the thing they are listening for is whether she will say 'obey' or not. It's no good trying to hear the bridegroom make the same vow because he has never done so. This has often been a point of friction and more often than not the problem has been solved by leaving the vow out altogether, but when it is used by the bride, the groom promises 'to worship'. So the wife obeys and the husband worships, but is this really right? The modern service has left it out altogether.

Obedience has to be a two-way experience. However much the husband might like his wife to be his humble servant, it is just not on. Obedience can of course be demanded, but if it is so important, it is a sure sign that the marriage is not based on love. Obedience comes naturally when there is mutual respect. When the husband respects his wife's knowledge, gifts and experience there will be many a time when he wants to obey her – and at other times the wife will have the same feelings about her husband. No one in a true partnership can have sole right to absolute obedience: it must be something that is shared. The days of 'What Dad says, goes' have gone but in its place is something far more exciting: the day of the partnership has very much dawned.

I love thee with the breath,
Smiles, tears, of all of my life! – and, if God choose,
I shall but love thee better after death.

Elizabeth Barrett Browning

Till death

Hankies are always very much in demand at weddings. The bridegroom's mother will have one neatly tucked up her sleeve, the bride's mother will come armed with a whole box of tissues. But there is a very strong possibility that the bride will have lost hers by the time she arrives at the chancel step. However, she may well need it more than anyone else, and the time she most needs it is when she says 'Till death do us part'.

That vow should always be at the back of our minds. The commitment that was undertaken on the wedding day is a commitment for life. It is not a commitment with small print that allows or encourages you to break it at any time. It is there until one of you dies. Sadly, many marriages – even those which started off with a firm intention of lasting the course – don't fulfil this commitment. This is part of the frailty of human nature. But many more do last and that must be a cause of thanksgiving. However we should always remember that we are only human. We will not last for ever and the day will come when either the husband or the wife has to say their last goodbye to their partner on this earth. More often than not it is the wife that is left, but, whichever partner it is, there is bound to be an emptiness and a loneliness. The person who has been by your side for so long is no longer physically with you. Then is the time for memories that wipe away the tears and the hope that in the life beyond you will be reunited.

Eggardon Hill Fort, Dorset.

My solemn vow

Making a vow must have a very solemn feel about it. You are after all giving your word, and that is a very precious thing to give. It is also something which is essentially very personal. At baptism services it is possible for someone to stand in for a Godparent who can't physically be there, to act as a proxy, but this certainly can't happen in the wedding service. Both parties have to be there and both parties have to agree fully with everything that is said, and the response to that agreement is to make a solemn vow.

When we were children we used to love promises. We loved making them, even in those days we were not too good at keeping them, and we loved receiving them, especially when they came from people we loved. That promise to take us to the park, the cinema or the beach on a Saturday was the thing that kept us going through the grind of the school week. Sometimes the promised treat might not come up to expectation but that didn't really matter, the promise had been kept. On those occasions when the promise was not kept then we felt let down or even, especially if it was something important, betrayed. And having been let down once there was the great fear that it could happen again.

The solemn vow made at the wedding is the most momentous promise that you can ever make. This is not the promise for a one-off treat, it is the promise of a life given to another for life, and there are no bigger promises than that.

With this ring

Wise ministers always have a curtain ring or something similar in their pocket just in case the best man has forgotten the wedding ring or, in handing it over, it slips off the prayer book and makes for the nearest grating. However, when the ring has been firmly placed on the prayer book and a blessing has been said over it, there is then the worry as to whether it will fit or not. Knuckles have a habit of swelling with excitement and nerves, which means that a ring which fitted so well in the jewellers now seems to be two sizes too small. But as the nerves calm down so the ring fits.

That band of gold, or whatever the ring is made of, is far more precious than the metal itself. It remains throughout your life the outward and visible sign that you are married. These days it is very common for the wife to give her husband a ring too so that both partners wear the symbol of their commitment to each other. The roundness of the ring acts as a symbol for the marriage itself: a marriage with edges can be a difficult and dangerous one; a marriage that has smoothed out all the edges is one that is set to last. The ring also serves as a symbol of eternity: the circle is endless just as the marriage is never-ending. And, finally, the precious metal can symbolise the preciousness of the relationship.

At major anniversaries couples often give each other another ring. It is always a good idea to have these rings blessed and so enjoy the chance to remind yourselves of those vows you took all those years ago.

With my body

The marriage service acknowledges that we are not just minds and spirits: we are bodies as well and how we treat our bodies is very important.

It is through our bodies that we physically relate to each other and so that kiss, that cuddle, that hug is such an important way of saying to one another 'I love you'. In Britain we are not particularly good about touching even those we love. We feel safe with a handshake but anything more than that is overstepping the mark. But that hand around the shoulder can be of such tremendous comfort to a person who is feeling a bit down. It shows that you are there with them in their suffering and are prepared to support them through it. The arms that are held open in greeting say more than any words that you are so glad to see them back again. And the hand held at the bedside of the dying partner shows that, whatever happens, it will not have to be faced alone.

The ultimate expression of love is when you totally commit yourselves to one another sexually. This should also be the greatest sign of respect for one another. It is where working in harmony is of paramount importance otherwise the desires of one partner are often satisfied at the expense of the other. Over the years the significance of the sexual side of the relationship will change, but despite the changes that physical relationship will still be the sign of total commitment.

The sexual embrace can only be compared with music and with prayer.

Havelock Ellis

All my worldly goods

There is a story that when a certain bridegroom was heard making the vow 'And with all my wordly goods I thee endow', someone was heard to say at the back of the church 'Oh good heavens! There goes his bicycle'.

The word that is now used during the wedding service instead of 'endow' is 'share', and it does seem far more appropriate. There are people who take one look at someone and think 'They would be a good catch'. This is not because they are beautiful or handsome, witty or understanding, it is because they have 'loads of money' and plenty of possessions. The relationship is then built on material gain rather than emotional input – yet it is meant to be a matter of sharing.

In any home there are bound to be things bought by one partner, but surely those things were bought for the enjoyment of both, not for the possession of one. The knowledge of what each other earns is not a way of controlling one another, it is a sign of trust and also a sign of sharing. You don't go to the fridge and note that you bought the butter and the salad while your partner bought the milk and the cheese. No: whatever is bought is for both of you to share. If it is a present that has been bought, then the enjoyment of both the giver and the receiver is there to be shared, for sharing is so much more thrilling than possessing.

River Tillingham Windmill, Rye.

Loders, Dorset.

The gift of children

The sadness couples experience who are not able to have children of their own or cannot adopt them is very great. They feel that they have been denied something, that they are unable to fulfil one of the most important of their wedding hopes. Some people decide for reasons of their own after much thought that they do not wish to have children. It is however very clearly stated in the marriage service that one of the most important reasons for getting married is so that you may receive the gift of children. This is a tremendous responsibility. On God's behalf you actually create a new being, and in that creation you strengthen the development and continuation of the human race. That may have been slightly hard to believe the first time you held the little bundle of humanity in your arms, but the creation of new life is a gift and like all gifts it must be used wisely.

Doubtless as the little bundles grew up into rather large packages you may have thought that they were a gift you could well do without, especially when they wouldn't do as they were told, when they actually defied you, when they wouldn't listen to your advice. But for the vast majority of parents the joy, the happiness and the fulfilment your children bring you outweigh the heartaches. You may feel distress on their behalf when life is difficult for them, but when you are surrounded by your children you realise that you have done the most wonderful thing anyone can do: you have created a new life.

If Heaven and Earth were not mated, the myriad things would not have been born. It is by means of the great rite of marriage that mankind subsists throughout the myriad generations.

Book of Rites

The wider family

The marriage of two people is the start of a new family or, as some people rather coldly say these days, a new unit. But it must never be an isolated unit for it has sprung from the roots of two families, and from the two families from which they sprang and so on. Now you may not be able to trace your family back to William the Conqueror and your house may not be recorded in the Domesday Book but there is every chance that you can go back a couple of generations.

Wise parents always make sure that when their children get married they are given room to breathe. But parents are very hurt if, having given them room to grow, their children decide to grow away from them and have very little to do with them. This is especially true when the grandchildren arrive. Children can benefit from knowing generations other than just their parents and normally there is no one better than a grandparent. Grans and Grandads may be liable to spoil the children but they can also be very wise friends and extremely good counsellors.

At one time, when everyone lived within easy reach, it was very easy for the family to keep in touch. Now that we often live miles apart we have to make a very definite effort to see each other, but it is an effort worth making. It is from our families that we draw our greatest support. When the chips are down, more often than not they are the ones we turn to. It is good that they share in our celebrations as well. And don't forget if the family is separated by the miles there is always the 'phone.

Coltishall, Norfolk.

Your place in society

Neighbours are not always good about calling when they see new people move into the street, or the block of flats – it's all part of the 'keeping yourself to yourself' syndrome. It's very understandable that they don't want to be nosey, even if they have kept an eye on the quality of the arriving furniture through the net curtains. But we do need to make people feel welcome and that they are part of a wider society.

This is so important for married couples. When they start their married life they can at times feel quite isolated. This isolation is naturally broken down when the children arrive and there are endless trips to clinics and then to schools. As the children join organisations like brownies, cubs, youth clubs and sports teams, wise parents also get themselves involved. Later on, when the children have grown up, the problem of isolation can re-appear. This is especially true if at your retirement you decide to move somewhere new so leaving the old friends and familiar faces behind. Now is the time to make sure that you are part of the wider society in your own right and not just as parents of your children. There are many groups you can join, there are lots of places to go where it is possible to meet others. With time at your disposal, it is good to keep an eye open for those who would benefit from your help and your company.

It is so important that at every stage of your marriage you don't keep yourselves to yourselves. You must make sure that you always take your rightful place in society.

Happy ever after

There is something wonderful about pantomimes. You always know that in the end everything will work out well. Prince Charming will find his Princess and even the wicked witch will have learnt the error of her ways. And the promise that everyone will live 'Happy ever after' sends you out of the theatre with hope in your heart and a spring in your step.

Real life marriages don't work like that. The family line-up for photographs after the ceremony may well resemble a pantomime but the guarantee of non-stop happiness is not given. However, it does need to be an inbuilt ingredient of any marriage. The ways in which that happiness is experienced can be very different. It can sometimes come out of great suffering, when you wondered how you were going to get through. But, because you faced that suffering together, when you did come through there was a feeling of great happiness. It may well come from the joy that you receive from your children. As they are thrilled with their achievements in life so their happiness becomes part of your happiness, spreading from person to person, from generation to generation.

None of us can expect to go through life on a cloud of joy: we have to face the realities of life. But we have to remember that happiness is as much a reality of life, and, just as troubles are halved when they are shared, so happiness is doubled especially when it is shared with the one you love.

> *The joys of marriage are the heaven on earth,*
> *Life's paradise, great princess, the soul's quiet.*
>
> John Ford

Appledore from Instow, Devon.

ISBN 0-7117-0525-0

Text copyright © 1990 Roger Royle
This edition copyright © Jarrold Publishing

Designed and produced by Parke Sutton Limited, Norwich for
Jarrold Publishing, Norwich

Printed in Portugal